Petworth
The Servants' Quarters

Smoking by Servants in Petworth House strictly prohibited.

LECONFIELD.

West Sussex

National Trust

The Servants' Quarters

The servants' block was rather like a production line. Food and other raw materials were delivered to the back door, and then stored and treated in a carefully planned series of larders, dairies and other service rooms until finally being prepared in the kitchens. At the opposite end, the business of the Estate was conducted in the estate offices, reached by a separate entrance and linked to the main house by a covered walkway. Upstairs, there are bedrooms for the staff, the female and male staff being at opposite ends, each with their own staircase. To be caught on the wrong staircase meant instant dismissal.

Rachel Sumpter, nurse, bathing a baby in the Nursery about 1890

Part of the *batterie de cuisine*: fish kettles on the top shelf and stockpots on the steam hotplate. Below is the oven

The Tunnel

Food, linen, coal and other necessities were carried across to the house by the footmen, housemaids and 'odd men' through an underground tunnel that connected the two buildings. (In the basement of the house itself were the butler's rooms — the plate-room, the wine and beer cellars, china store and oil- and lamp rooms.) In this way, the noise and smells of cooking were kept well away from the family's own rooms, as was the risk of fire. For the servants, however, it meant that the long distances travelled through corridors and tunnels were their abiding memory of Petworth.

History

The servants' block was built in the mid-18th century and is shown as it would have looked between 1920 and 1940, little changed from Victorian times. A severe fire in the kitchens in 1872 resulted in the refitting of many of the rooms, and in 1891 the extension of the northern end provided new men's bedrooms and storerooms. Few further changes were made through to the 1930s, when there were still around 35 indoor servants, plus daily help as required. At the outbreak of the Second World War in 1939, the Petworth staff moved into the main house to make way for the Chelsea Day Nursery evacuated from London. Only seven staff remained throughout the war, some of whom were allowed to sleep in grand bedrooms on the first floor of the main house.

In 1947 Petworth was given to the National Trust by Charles Wyndham, 3rd Lord Leconfield, who continued to live in the house, as his heirs do today. The servants' block was never fully

reoccupied by the family's staff after the war and was used mostly for storage. In 1995 the kitchens were opened to the public for the first time, and as much as possible of the splendid copper *batterie de cuisine* was brought down from the attics. With other original contents generously loaned by Lord and Lady Egremont, and the help of former members of staff, it has been possible to re-create a very accurate picture of life in the Servants' Quarters.

The Upper Servants' Dining Room in 1925

3

The Upper Servants

Joseph Pattinson,
house steward, 1881–99.
Photographed in 1894,
when he was 61

Mrs Rawlinson,
housekeeper, 1884–91

At the head of the establishment was the house steward, who worked directly for Lord Leconfield and supervised the indoor staff. He was responsible for paying the bills at the family's London and other residences, as well as at Petworth. In today's terms, he was running a sizeable business, with monthly bills totalling £1,000 in the 1890s.

The house steward was a 'gentleman', who did not wear a uniform and 'lived out' in a spacious house in the grounds, although Lord Leconfield laid down that, 'if I find it necessary, I may compel him to sleep in the house'. Other staff were paid 'sleeping money' to stay overnight in the house. Joseph Pattinson was the last house steward at Petworth, and on his retirement in 1899 the position of butler assumed many of the steward's responsibilities. These included directing the under-butlers, usher, footmen, odd men and steward's-room man, as well as looking after the wine and beer cellars and the plate, receiving visitors and serving at table.

The house steward controlled the entire enterprise, hiring additional staff as required and overseeing all purchases. Listed in Pattinson's accounts are tickets for the theatre, buckskin gloves for the footmen, plate powder, ginger beer for a cricket match, pipes and tobacco for the servants' party, violin strings, beetle powder, oranges, cherries and a fishing rod box. He also paid the poulterer, the butterman, the butcher, fishmonger, greengrocer, milkman and baker, and arranged for pianos to be tuned, boots mended, chimneys swept and clocks wound. Harvey and Nichols, W.H. Smith & Co., Robert McVitie and Twinings appear in the accounts, as does HM Prison Portsmouth, which supplied the house with mops.

The other upper servants were the chef and the housekeeper, who, with the lady's maid, valet and governess, lived and worked mainly in the house. Both chef and housekeeper had their own rooms in the servants' block and their own teams of staff. Discipline and standards were strictly maintained by the senior staff, who tended to remain in post for between five and 25 years, whilst the housemaids and footmen moved frequently seeking promotion.

Wages

In the 1890s the chef and butler were paid £120 per annum — with the valet, the next most highly paid member of staff, earning £70. The housekeeper was the highest paid female member of staff and earned £50. Wages for footmen ranged between £22 and £40, and for housemaids between £10 and £25. In addition, staff received monthly allowances for beer or tea and for washing and board wages to buy food when the family was away. Those who lived in also had free accommodation.

Livery

The male indoor staff, the coachmen, huntsmen and lodgekeepers were provided with a uniform, known as livery. Footmen received a 'courier' jacket (blue with silver crested buttons), a striped waistcoat, a pair of black trousers and calico drawers, a 'morning jacket', a greatcoat and a hat, gloves, stockings and pumps. In 1873 the annual cost of full livery was £34 for the under-butler and £32 for a footman. The female staff generally provided their own uniforms.

A Petworth housemaid in her morning working clothes. The female staff wore print or grey dresses with aprons and black stockings in the mornings, and black dresses with aprons, hats and black stockings in the afternoons

Alfred Lee, T. Reed and William Watts, footmen, 1904–5

The Estate Servants

The stable yard staff in 1884. Note the initials 'LL' (for Lord Leconfield) on the bucket

The garden staff with their tools in the 1880s. The head gardener with his bowler hat sits in the middle. The donkey was used to draw the great roller

(*Opposite*) Dan Crawley, gunsmith, Jim Reed, blacksmith, and George Simpson, from the estate yard, stoking up the fire pump during a practice in 1940. Their gas-masks are in the shoulder bags

Petworth House was the centre of a considerable estate, which included land in Yorkshire and the Lake District and property in London. The valet, lady's maid, footmen, chef and kitchen staff would travel with the family between their houses, leaving the housekeeper, housemaids and occasionally the house steward at Petworth. After the racing at Goodwood each summer, the family would move to Cockermouth Castle in Cumberland in August, returning to Petworth for Christmas, and then spending three months in London in the spring.

At Petworth itself, there were 24 grooms and coachmen in the stables, 25 gardeners and many more on the estate. The house also had its own fire brigade, engine and pump. The servants' block even included a room for an upholsterer and for a professional cricketer, perhaps employed to coach the estate team.

Although many local suppliers relied on business from the house, Petworth was virtually self-sufficient. The park provided venison, game, eels and fish, the last being

moved to specially built stewponds above the lake in order to lose their muddy taste before being brought into the Kitchen. The eels were sometimes placed in the fountain on the south lawn. Meat, eggs and poultry came from the home farm at Stag Park, while the extensive kitchen gardens produced fruit and vegetables, and flowers and plants for decorating the house. The gardens were famous for growing 400 varieties of vegetables and 100 kinds of pear.

Fred Streeter, head gardener from 1929 to 1947, recalled that his first task on arriving at Petworth was to interview the kitchen garden foreman, who complained:

> I don't know how it's possible to grow enough for that lot. There are so many departments — there's the dining room, the steward's room, the housemaids, the pantry and the servants' hall, besides the kitchens. It's like feeding a factory. And there's the outsiders.

He soon regulated the deliveries of vegetables from the gardens and built up a new and harmonious relationship with the cook. He continued the tradition of supplying Lord Leconfield with his daily 'violet' or bunch of eight tiny radishes, eight spring onions and a cucumber.

Close to the servants' block lay the cowyard, which once contained the milking sheds, piggery, dairy, game larder and ice-houses. In the woodyard, just outside the Kitchen windows, there was the brewhouse, bakehouse, fuel stores and battery house for electric power, together with the laundry, which moved to a new site in 1873.

6

The Kitchen Equipment

In this one room, cooking styles spanning 300 years can be seen. After the 1872 fire, the Kitchen was refitted with the latest in cooking technology, but retained the traditional roasting range in front of the great fireplace, which probably incorporates brickwork from the Tudor kitchens. Producing on average 100 meals a day and sometimes three or four times that number, the Petworth kitchens were comparable in scale to those of a major hotel.

Roasting

In Elizabethan times, the spits of the roasting range had been turned by 'Harrye the kitchen boy'. Later, they were turned by a large fan in the chimney, which was driven by the heat and smoke of the fire. A skilled roasting chef would control the proximity of the food to the fire and also adjust the size of the fire itself by cranking the handle that moves the sliding cheeks in and out. A huge dripping pan underneath caught the fat, which could be used for basting with the long-handled ladles. The trolley opposite warmed dishes and also kept some of the heat of the fire out of the Kitchen. A former kitchenmaid remembers that 'when the fire was going full tilt, the Kitchen was absolutely stifling'.

Steaming

The latest innovation in 1872 was steam-powered cooking apparatus, and in this kitchen there are warming ovens, a hotplate, steamers and a *bain-marie*, all fed by a huge steam-raising boiler in the Scullery. Running along the inside wall can be seen the hot closet with hotplate over, on which three stockpots provide a constant supply of fish, meat and vegetable stock for the numerous sauces cooking gently in the *bain-marie* opposite. Next to the oven and hotplate after the dresser are the vegetable and meat steamers and boilers – large square copper boxes with a steam inlet pipe at the back, tap in front and condensing hood above. These were also used for cooking steamed and Christmas puddings.

Gas

Underneath the windows a gas stove was fitted in the 1920s to replace earlier charcoal stoves. Breakfast was prepared here: one large pan full of eggs, another of bacon, others with boiled eggs, kedgeree (made with salmon or turbot), and two kettles to provide a ready supply of hot water.

Electricity

The most modern pieces of equipment are the 1940s Aga-type solid fuel 'Gloworm' range and the 1920s Benham electric ovens next to the door to the Scullery. The electric ovens were used to make the family's scones for breakfast, amongst other things.

The 1920s gas range

Tall saucepans, tinned inside and out, stand in the hot water of the *bain-marie*, their contents carefully labelled

(*Opposite*) The long central deal table is the main working area in the Kitchen

The Kitchen Staff

Annie Monk, kitchenmaid, 1888–91

The chef was the master of the kitchens and in the 1870s and 1880s was assisted from time to time by a pastry chef and a roasting chef (usually all French), as well as two or three kitchenmaids and a scullery man. Each had their allotted work space on the large central table: in 1937 the chef worked with his back to the windows at the end nearest the fire, with the head kitchenmaid facing him, and the two kitchenmaids at the other end facing each other. Highly valued for his expertise and skill, the chef concentrated on the more difficult and spectacular dishes, the numerous sauces and dressings, leaving the others to prepare the simpler parts of the family's and servants' meals.

Life in the Kitchen

First to arrive at about 6am was the junior kitchenmaid, who began by cleaning out and relighting the fire before taking a cup of tea to the chef and the head kitchenmaid. Preparations then began in earnest for breakfast, which was taken at 8am by the staff and at 9 by the family. Other tasks for the junior kitchenmaid in the mornings included making yeast buns for the staff afternoon tea and cleaning the Chef's Sitting Room and Bedroom and the bedrooms of the other kitchenmaids. Meanwhile, the chef, dressed in his best clothes, would visit Lady Leconfield to discuss the day's menus, having given instructions to the other kitchen staff on the preparations needed for lunch. This was the main meal of the day, taken by the staff at 12.15 and the family at 1. The menu books show that, whilst the family's meals were elaborate, those for the Servants' Hall were just as plentiful. Former staff at Petworth are almost unanimous in declaring the food to have been excellent: roasts on Tuesdays, Thursdays and Sundays, rabbits twice a week, and plenty of cakes and buns.

After cleaning the kitchens and scrubbing the stone floor, there was some free time after lunch before preparations for tea and dinner began. One under-kitchenmaid recalled that if there had been a shooting party staying in the house, it could be after midnight before she had finished her work, and 'on such occasions the chef would bring out his bottle of punch and give us a drink and we'd feel very much part of a team'.

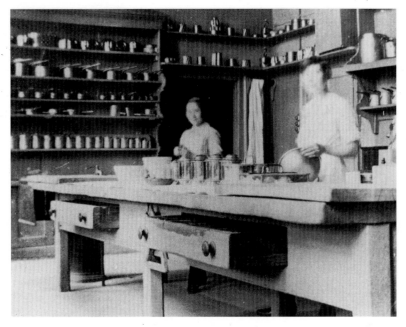

The Kitchen in 1929. This photograph was used as a guide for the display of the *batterie de cuisine*

Elaborate confections such as these triple-layered jellies were produced in the Petworth kitchens

1. Dinner is served in the *Square Dining Room* by the footmen, overseen by the under-butler

2. Footmen hurry through the *underground tunnel* carrying the dishes covered by domed meat covers and blankets

3. Next to the Housekeeper's Room, the *Still Room* provided coffee, tea, juices, pickles and preserves

4. The cool *Pastry* offered ideal working conditions for the pastry chef's special confections

5. In the *Kitchen* the chef works at the table assisted by the kitchenmaids, while watching over the meats roasting in front of the open fire

6. In the *Scullery* the scullery man holds a salamander over a pie to brown it, while the kitchenmaids help to prepare vegetables and clean the copper cooking pots

7. The *Chef's Sitting Room* was a welcome refuge from the hustle and bustle of the kitchens

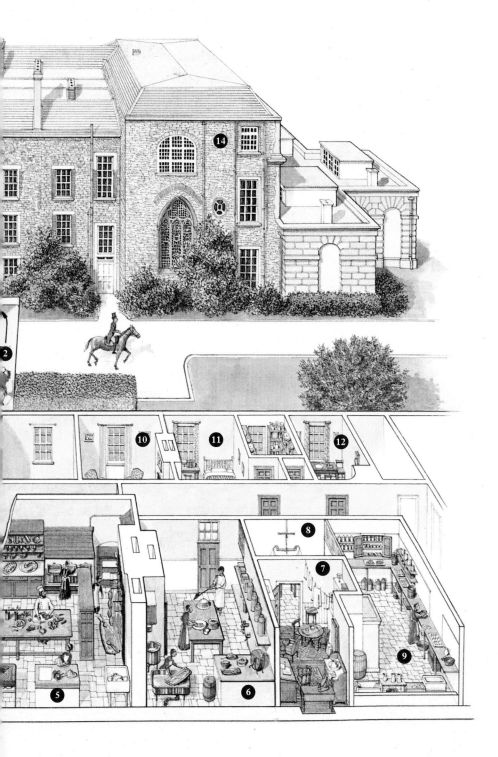

8 In the *Weighing Room* the chef checked supplies coming into the Larder

9 Away from the heat of the kitchens, the *Larder* is a cool room where food and dry goods could be stored securely

10 In the *Housemaids' Sitting Room* tasks were allocated daily after breakfast by the head housemaid

11 The *Chef's Bedroom*, with a small china store adjacent, is close to the kitchens

12 The *Steward's Office* overlooked all arrivals and deliveries to the back door

13 *Bedrooms* for the male staff were at the northern end of the first floor, while the housekeeper and female staff slept at the southern end

14 The *attics* of the main house provided bedrooms for the visiting staff and for the lady's maid, valet, governess and nurserymaids

The Pastry

Away from the heat of the main kitchen, the Pastry provided ideal working conditions for making pies, biscuits, cakes and pastries. (A separate bakehouse in the woodyard behind baked the bread for the house.) It is a room carefully designed for ease of operation. A large high window provides good light for the main working area – the large marble slab. On the left-hand side is a cupboard for spices, sugar, dried fruits and tins, whilst on the right are the drawers for rolling pins and cutters, with flour bins underneath and a worktop above. The rack holds twelve copper baking trays, and the cupboard now displays the collection of plain and fluted, dome-topped and ornamental-shaped darioles (round moulds), quenelle moulds and tinplate baking tins. Note the tinned quenelle moulds in the shape of jockey caps, hams, eggs and strawberries.

In the lobby outside the Pastry is the old pastry oven which was heated by bundles of lit twigs. Once the oven was hot, the pies and pastries could be put in and the door sealed shut until they were cooked – a judgement requiring great skill and experience. This oven was superseded by the electric ovens in the main kitchen and was only recently rediscovered.

In the 1870s and 1880s a pastry chef, usually French, worked in here. From the 1890s onwards fewer male cooks were employed, replaced by more skilled kitchen-maids, and often the chef himself would use the Pastry to make more complicated confections. Blackcurrant leaves were supplied from the kitchen garden to flavour the pastry.

Richard Grant, chef from 1931 to 1937, was very secretive when he was working in the Pastry and is remembered for his skill at icing and decorating cakes and for a special coronation cake that featured bunches of roses lit by tiny bulbs.

Richard Grant, chef from 1931 to 1937, photographed at Cockermouth Castle

(*Above left*) A 'cook's confection' in sugar paste of the 1880s

(*Opposite*) The oven in the Pastry Lobby was heated by bundles of twigs, which were then raked out into the ash pit below

15

The Scullery

Dominating the room is the magnificent late 19th-century low-pressure twin-flue steam boiler by Messrs Jeakes & Co. This produced steam for the apparatus in the Kitchen and steam to the circular copper nearby to heat the water.

Both the sink and the circular copper have two water supplies: river water for washing pots, pans and vegetables, and well water for drinking and cooking. There is a deep well in the centre of the courtyard (reached by the underground tunnel), which provided the clean water. A beam pump on the River Rother, 1½ miles south of Petworth at Coultershaw, produced the second supply. The Coultershaw water engine is in full working order and open to the public. Mineral water in barrels costing five shillings each was purchased two or three times a week when the family was at Petworth. This was an understandable precaution, as the 2nd Lord Leconfield's son George had died of typhoid in 1895. Above the circular copper is a Winser & Co. Ltd 60-gallon patent cistern, which periodically flushed the Kitchen drains.

The scullery man's day was long, starting at 6am and lasting until 10pm, with a break in the afternoon. As well as cleaning all the copper pans with a mixture of salt, sand and vinegar and keeping the boiler in working order, he helped the cook to joint carcasses of meat and prepared rabbits, hares, pheasant, chicken, quails and snipe for the Kitchen. Deliveries of vegetables brought up from the gardens daily in a large wheelbarrow were washed before being taken into the Kitchen. Mr Baigent, scullery man in the 1920s and 1930s, also made the ice-cream and cleaned the eels that were Lord Leconfield's particular favourite,

hanging them up on the pipes in the Scullery. His speciality was Baked Alaska, the meringue being cooked by holding a red-hot salamander — a long iron pole with a square metal head set diagonally — over the frothy egg whites. The chef would sometimes model the meringue into the shape of a bird, which was browned with the salamander.

Above the doors leading out of the Scullery are ham and bacon lofts. The large flat hooks on the wall near the top of the Kitchen door are for storing spare spits for the roasting range.

The knife polisher

Unused for 50 years, the steam boiler was still full of ash and water when it came to be conserved in 1994

Bacon could be hung for up to a year in this loft and hams in the loft opposite

The Scullery

17

The Chef's Sitting Room and Weighing Room

The chef was responsible for the smooth running of the kitchens. He had to find his own kitchenmaids, subject to Lady Leconfield's approval, and he also took on extra cooks, charwomen and a scullery man at Petworth and appointed kitchen staff for the London house. Local suppliers tended to be specified by Lord Leconfield and the house steward, but the chef could order extra delicacies such as turtle soup, truffles, lobster, turbot, sole, oysters and some spices. Outside his office is the Weighing Room where deliveries could be checked before being stored in the Larder.

A French chef of the 1880s

A page from Chef Nolot's account book of 1881

A bill of 1885 for 'best clear Turtle and Green Fat'

Expensive and unusual items would be kept in his own room in the lockers along the wall.

The position of chef seems to have become increasingly difficult to fill, with most incumbents in the 1890s remaining for less than a year. Between chefs a female cook stood in, earning £70 per annum — considerably less than a French chef but more than the housekeeper. The skills of a good cook were highly prized.

In 1900 Charles Grosstephan became cook and stayed for eleven years, to be succeeded by Signor Michelle Milone, who had come to England in the retinue of Prince Louis of Battenburg. His daughter, Violet Margaret, left this description of him:

> A chef by profession, though his habiliments [dress] of bowler hat, black coat and rolled umbrella could easily have dubbed him a 'City Gent'. But we knew better, for secreted in various pockets were the choicest of leftovers ... — charlotte russe, leg of chicken, gooey gateaux — brought to us at night when we were abed.

After another unsettled period in the kitchens, Mrs Lane was appointed cook in 1927 on the same salary as her male predecessors. A few of her recipes survive. In 1931 she was replaced by Richard Grant, who stayed for seven years, until a French chef returned to Petworth again in the shape of Monsieur Chassagne. In August 1940 Mrs Miles took over and remained as cook throughout the war.

The cook had a bedroom on the opposite side of the corridor, next to the China Room. The cook's office was used as a combined dining- and sitting-room by all the kitchen staff in the 1930s.

The Chef's Sitting Room

The Larder

Ice-cream moulds in
the Larder

Originally, it was the main larder for the Kitchen. In 1873 this northern end of the servants' block was extended to provide a separate Meat Larder and Winter Dairy. The Larder then became a general-purpose food preparation and storage area, essentially a dry larder with salting equipment.

To work well, a larder should be cool, dry and well-ventilated. This room is ideally sited at the north-east corner of the building, with windows which were at one time fitted with wire gauze to keep out insects, and panels of wire gauze in the door and around the room to improve air circulation. The walls are whitewashed and tiled to aid cleaning, and the stone-flagged floor had a drain.

The slate shelving provides a cold surface for standing bowls, pitchers and baskets, and underneath are the large egg-preserving bowls, still with traces of the lime used to preserve the eggs. Behind the door is a large pestle and mortar for grinding patés. The two slate troughs under the windows were for salting whole sides of pork, which were then hung from the hooks in the ceiling.

The ice-box is an early refrigerator: large blocks of ice were placed on one side, and pies, cold cooked meats, fish and cheeses on the other. It is zinc-lined and tiled for insulation. The ice-house is close to the back door of the servants' block and is divided into three enormous pits to provide a constant supply of ice.

The red-brick building that can be seen from the windows of the Larder is the Battery House, so called because it once contained two large gas engines on the ground floor generating electricity for the house and the town which was stored in batteries on the first floor.

Ice-cream

No Victorian meal was complete without an ice-cream or ice dessert. The cupboard contains a remarkable collection of pewter and tin ice-cream moulds found at Petworth. Elaborate baskets of coloured fruits made from ice-cream could be created or plainer Neapolitan ice-creams made in the block moulds. The hinged two-piece pewter individual fruit moulds are in the shapes of an apple, an artichoke, asparagus bundles, baskets of flowers, a fig, grapes, a melon, an orange, a pear, a pineapple (with or without leaves on top), a rose, a strawberry and a walnut.

Making ice-cream was a complicated and lengthy process. Firstly, a custard of cream, sugar, colourings and flavourings was poured into the pewter freezing pots with the convex bases, which were then placed into buckets full of ice and saltpetre. The flat ice spatulas were used to stir the mixture periodically until the ice-cream was formed. This could take up to three hours and was another duty of the scullery man. The ice-cream mixture was then put into the mould and further frozen until it was time to be served.

The Still Room

Opposite the entrance to the Kitchen is the Still Room, which had its own maids and was under the control of the housekeeper, whose sitting-room adjoined. It was here that all bottling and preserving took place, and jams, marmalades and pickles were stored. The still-room maids also produced tea, coffee and all soft drinks and fruit juices, including lemon barley water for the tennis matches in the 1930s. More exotic preparations included prunes bottled in gin, strawberries in champagne, and candied and preserved fruit. The housekeepers' account books record regular purchases of brandy, which was probably infused with fruits, herbs and spices before being strained and bottled. Two hundredweight of black currants were supplied from the kitchen garden each year, and white currants dipped in sugar were also served as a dessert.

The Still Room's second important function was to make the early morning tea trays for family and guests. Tea or coffee with toast or a scone was exquisitely presented on special trays decorated with nosegays brought up from the gardens. In the 1930s Lord Leconfield enjoyed a jar of Gentleman's Relish on his early morning tray. In the afternoon, china and cakes for tea were put out.

The still-room maids were responsible for the special china — the dessert services and delicate pieces. They would wash them carefully standing on a coir mat to minimise the risk of breakage, if anything should accidentally fall. Running the Still Room required special skills, and the maids were often paid more than the housemaids and kitchenmaids, and wore their own clothes.

The housekeeper

The housekeeper was also responsible for the china and linen stores and for the laundrymaids and housemaids at London and Petworth. She did not move with the family between houses, but stayed at Petworth to supervise the annual spring cleaning. She also made regular visits to the family's London house to check on the house staff and make special purchases. The housekeepers' accounts show mostly travel expenses for trips between London and Petworth, washing allowances paid to the housemaids, and postage costs.

The housekeepers at Petworth were always addressed as 'Mrs' as a mark of respect (whether married or not). They stayed in the post for considerable periods: Mrs Forty for fourteen years from 1893 to 1907, and Mrs Cownley for 25 years until 1933. Mrs Cownley is remembered as kindly and motherly towards the young housemaids. She was fond of hats, played bridge with her visitors, and kept a store of jigsaws for her younger guests.

Gertrude Holgate, senior still-room maid, 1904–8

Mrs Cownley (by the sewing machine) with other Petworth staff working as Red Cross nurses in the Audit Room during the First World War

The Still Room. Over the fireplace is a portrait of Mrs Purser, housekeeper until 1814